FINISHING LINE PRESS
www.finishinglinepress.com

The Dreamed

poems by

Nancy Devine

Finishing Line Press
Georgetown, Kentucky

The Dreamed

ACKNOWLEDGMENTS

Poem "20" originally appeared as **Prairie opens her two cupped hands** in
Hobble Creek Review issue 2 volume 3.

Publisher: Leah Maines

Editor: Christen Kincaid

Cover Art: https://unsplash.com/license

Author Photo: Charles Devine

Cover Design: Nancy Devine

Printed in the USA on acid-free paper.
Order online: www.finishinglinepress.com
              also available on amazon.com

Author inquiries and mail orders:
Finishing Line Press
P. O. Box 1626
Georgetown, Kentucky 40324
U. S. A.

Table of Contents

Poems are numbered and appear as follows:

"The Dreamed" is for the part of us that endures beyond loss as well as for those that guide us through it.

Mercutio: That dreamers often lie.
Romeo: In bed asleep, while they do dream things true.
(From Shakespeare's *Romeo and Juliet*)

1

If my brother was saying, "look ma, no hands,"
when he walked into the river,
or no feet or heart,
even mind and atmosphere,
I can't keep loving him as though he were
alive. He could swim;
I can swim, even if I don't want to anymore.

"Thread water. How can you thread water?"
No tread.
"But can't you make the river weave between your fingers?
If you just put your
hand in it, that's how the water goes."

2

We didn't have a name for what our brother was except
brother and all our father knew was
son. Then it was not son and our brother
began his long silences, the eternity
that follows the drum beat of death or
when you don't know what to call yourself
in that soft whisper before sleep.

Did my brother want other boys?
Did he wish he weren't a boy?
Did he hear voices?
Did the voices cough and sputter?
Was he afraid of light?
The press of its heavy hand?
What? Can't the river tell us something other than wet
and wave and gurgle and spit?

I have a lifetime
to get these questions unanswered,
to cube and square them,
to graph and hate them.

Was he really not my father's son?
To whom could he have belonged
if not the river? What about
us? Us?

3

What our brother spit out was
dream, ragged spittle on the sidewalk
chalked with recess games;
mother put the afternoon away:
the sun in its block,
the glasses in their wood.

I could not stand the heat
our cold north turned inside out,
unabashed about the structure of its mesentery.

I never prayed about this or any
other thing is what I often said.
What incantation gets someone to exit
his psychosis? Teach it to me now:
I will practice it as a jump-rope chant,
the whack of the rope on the cement
my metronome, my feet there
the beats between beats,
a syncopation to my heart. The girls
holding and twirling the ends, I
will be both of them, keeping steady
with a hand on my hip.

4

In one spot, the river is calm,
gentle like any slough where my brother and father would hunt ducks,
the mallards' heads green as rhubarb leaves—that supposed poison.

The bank is soft but firm enough to hold the weight of a man,
one who might've gotten off his bike on the nearby trail
and walked down to the water to pause or think,
not of consequence or cause,
but of how surprising it is to find beauty in a place
without special designation or marking.

(I wanted to be soft once, that my body
would give to certain touch I've never named).

This is not where my brother walked in.

He was near a bridge,
where the water spins and roils near its base
like storm clouds fighting before drowning
in it, surface tension a malaise of movement.
He went in near huge cylindrical shaped masses of cement
whose skeleton is re-rod.
There cottonwoods stretch from shore,
leaves rubbing together in wind
like a thousand hands trying to get warm,
their roots extending down through soil
like caissons supporting grid work
that gets people from one shore to the other,
though he was not near them…
the woman tugging at her purse,
the girls skipping school,
one having her early in the day smoke.

5

Perfume and cologne coated the mourners like icing on a ganache,
silky-looking like a cement floor floated perfectly.
So many so low-built to the ground I remember thinking when
I looked out into the narthex from the small all-red chapel
where we waited. Jesus beamed around us in colored glass
in an oil painting of him on a hill with sheep,
a portrait, his senior picture for that grand year-book
about to be quoted from, invoked, exulted.

We entered the sanctuary as one flock flocked with tears;
the congregation stood to look at us, tally our manner of sorrow.
Our father stood at the door to the church sanctuary a long time
before filing in with the family.

When we sat in our pew, he was the last,
as if he were hanging on to a rag of a story just outside his reach.
The thing is it was a different story than the rest of us wanted.
But we just didn't know, at least in the way
that knowing is usually done…(did I mention?)
with the words and the phrases
that hang together sensibly as sentences
and then whole pages that become beginning, middle and end,
in that order….not end strangling middle just as she is beginning.

It's all a mess, I know….beyond the telling of it.

6

In the last dream of my brother,
when sleep secured itself in the castle of my mind,
I watched myself get up.
I passed through our house
and walked to the medicine cabinet in the main floor bathroom
and looked at myself.
But then it wasn't me, but my brother…
how I had remembered him….pale, spongy,
and I noticed how our faces are the same,
what has become after so much.

Then I sunk back down below the level of my dreams
where catfish graze the bottom's silt like earthworms who
digest and expel soil, oxygenated if only
you have the gills or guts to breathe it.

My brother would say to me,
"the people who make your art
are not in the sun right now;
they are not drinking a daiquiri
from a breast-shaped glass.
They are inside working
in the factory of their house or apartment
alone, mostly, sometimes stopping to think more
and then less. Someone like me
is not art. But you can make art of me, later, if
you wish, my skin the hide of a canvas,
my bones notes ossified. And you'll will. "

God, how I wish I understood the soon-ness of later,
the frightening way it is first too much light
and then unrestrained dark, black emesis.
In neither do
I find my brother. Trust me I have looked and…
seam-ripper in my left hand.
And what I ask you brother who wanted to be
the Titanic, a bottom-feeder who rose
to the surface north of us, what will my
art be today if it can't be you?

8

We thought the man married to the mother of a girl in our dance class
was not her father. The whole town did, though no one said in public.
The many things no one said in public then could fill a stadium with
pure decay, like collected road kill spread across a hot parking lot,
    scavenger
birds perennially tethered to their nests.

She twirled batons and her hair, the corkscrew curls that hung
alongside her face, like crystals from a chandelier. Where
her siblings were ugly, their faces lumpy clay not-yet-molded,
she was a beautiful, freckled butterfly that we were supposed
to hate.

I threatened to go door to door to check everyone's **World Book
    Encyclopedia**
to see which pages were dog-eared or oily in a spot where the fingers
kept touching with disbelief. I wanted to lie into the phone,
spit into the ropy wires that spanned our town.

I said I'd call every number and ask whoever answered just who they
    thought
our brother was and wasn't.

My mother said people didn't have the words;
she said it with the nonchalance
one would expect if she'd said,
"no dear, they don't have outdoor pools."

As I was saying…
Once he exited his psychoses, things got better.
Sure they did. Iced tea sweet brown in high ball glasses
cylindrical enough for hand, for drink….that kind of
better…I was saying.
Petit fours for the three of us,
crudités, pate, hip-hip hooray
we chanted from our play house.
You do this when you're a kid,
stupid as sheep or a moth who
wants its wing on light just to
prove the antithesis of burn.
Our father changing—
the silver coin supplants that
close, an eye medallion
caboose-soldered to track,
a porcelain pig's belly engorged enough
to burst piñata style
and my brother's the blind-folded kid.
Our mother inside turning the pot
instead of the spoon.

10

And there was the part we came to call
more…as in *more of it*. We didn't know what it was,
just a growing that left us little room in that house.

Silence…he'd go to his room for hours,
leave the door cracked so we would hear
but not go in, see but not touch.
I had to look up the word *flagellate*.
Then I looked up everything….lampshades,
trees dressed in too much snow.
And, as you might imagine, everything
began to look down at me,
the drain of my mouth,
the pea trap of my gut.
This is when I started to say nothing.

Hey, isn't it impossible to imagine
your way back into the past?
(Not that you won't get there.) You might not
be able to get back here with its shuttered windows
that scare away the light, and hidden under an eyelid
striped retractable awnings
beneath which a family gathers to pray,
to spit into the wind,
one in the same most days except.
Thursday—it was a Thursday—when
a fat brindle rabbit
glowed under a car
parked across the street,
a car where a neighbor boy and his cross-town girl
tried to turn their tingling surfaces into one
foreplay's fast fusion,
without shunning trousers, thong, brief,
where they kissed and moaned, glowed
and giggled at the funniest joke with a punch line
none of us over here remembers or has known.

Past-present-and-future merely
a continuum of walk
under a covered bridge,
rain pelting the metal,
some teeth sowed by a wicked hand.

Not us over here; we like to drown
to die. We melt the snow from our backyard
in a huge mouth-shaped cauldron. It's
bubbling like some sugar syrup approaching
the soft ball stage still. This is when we wade in.

12

Okay right. you've got the gun and it feels surprisingly oily.
What you see, that screen that butts up against your eyes—
a change that's not going to change—that's not what you want.
But you don't want the silence no one has written of,
the water slamming over us like a heavy box shut.
It's something that has its appeal. You look askance,
try it to catch it out of the corner of your eye,
an actor entering the stage whose ends are your periphery.
You put the gun away. You don't really put it away,
because you don't have a gun.
You are deathly afraid of guns.
Why not this, dear brother? Why not?

13

I've a river inside me, she says. We lie on the bed,
our feet hanging over its edge as though it's a barge
and we are just kids floating along in the summer,
the sun in love with and afraid of us at the same time.

When I tried to picture the channel of her body,
dark water moving along in it,
muddy banks for her hips I could not bear it,

Maybe that's what our mother thought—
thought when she lay in her bed
and looked out the window,
the mouth inevitable
spilling into some ocean one's only fate.

14

That summer my sister wrote 400 poems, or so she said.
I read only 30, including the one I remember—
I lay on a beach towel in our backyard, coconut
sun tan lotion on my back, my sister under the hood
of a dying elm and her gray sweatshirt.

I am the unimagined manifest,
what shadows slough at day's end,
also....the stitching of a shroud,
the hem of my mother's mouth
when the needle is flourished one last time,
like a Roman Candle low.

If you think me other, you are wrong.
I am other's other, its self-made twin,
Whatever isn't banished to the grave
I just am.

This on the back of an envelope for a bill
from the phone company.

No one ever figured I'd be the child to make
paper a friend…So all this is
a party. No cake. Only favors.

15

The morning my brother walked into the river,
my mother was singing. This, of course, is something
we can only know now…now as we try to be
the book end of this side of the story.

Did she crescendo as the water got as deep
as his shoulders, breathe between phrases
as he disappeared under the river's dun surface?
He was sad for years; Thursday should not have been a surprise.
My sister and I had been harmonizing with our mother,
finding the descant
above the melody, like tip-toeing across a pond in the throes of
    freeze-thaw,
what you can hold onto
so you won't go down.

But we did what we did.

That?

I don't remember.

16

And to carry someone each day extra makes you heavy,
so if you swim,
you sink or you must tread harder than machine guns and
bomb sprayers ruining our world one pass at a time
even through what's inevitable and worse.
I drag my limbs with me from room to room;
they are the friends I have.
If you recognize me somehow, smile; I am not unfriendly.
I've been known to wave.

Now each object has too much import.
What is behind
an empty cup on a saucer near a crust of toast,
a mitten dropped on the floor?
Because before, everyday
buckles and belts
screamed in sloppy code:
I will walk into the river,
and for a while,
all of you will forget how to swim.

So my mother turns over to face
the open window as she sleeps, but she is not sleeping;
the breeze banks off her brow. I want to bend
to her comfort her. I pretend she is sleeping.
It is something for both of us that week
or was it the week after?
Is love when we give each other what we have
even if we have something?

My sister haunts the hallway, my father
weeps in his office. Some of the bills paid
have tear stains across the amount due.
But the checks get cashed and no one mentions
the irony of it. We have lights, water, groceries and
insurance. Can you believe it. Oh, yes…electricity.

18

In the late afternoon in the tea of day,
when our clothes clung to us like drowning friends,
the sun so hot it just stood there in the room with us,
that's when mother disappeared beyond the scrim of herself.

My sister never saw it: how the hand of our mother
reached in through the head of our mother
and pulled our other mother out,
while our father's gin gimlet gurgled its glass,
the brother we wished we didn't have lolled
on the front porch as if some breeze or lesser wind
might help.

I regret the seas of years that passed like that,
how I was just vapor or was I dream?

Every time I drink or swallow,
I can't imagine what mother... I'll bring out
from myself.

19

Prairie opens her two cupped hands.
Studebaker fins just
and angle; they are the color of eggplant,
dusty eggplant.
Latticework frames the doorway,
rising and falling so many times
it's no longer the house's feeble try at resurrection.

I've painted my legs with fake tanner,
ensconced them in flannel pajamas. *I want*
to wake different is what I used to think,
my thighs shades of burnished orange rinds,

my hands symmetrical
like the car in the driveway
leaking some auto
amniotic fluid onto the pocked cement
in the shape of a cloud, a particular
one roiled with rain in
the western sky where
I imagined this town ends and
the next thing over is its hearse.

20

A moment is like the end of a megaphone where the mouth goes
and says its deal. The shape that follows is everything,
before it increasing steadily in circumference
until the megaphone ends and stretches simultaneously out
to include the whole damned world.

All I have is my lips conceding to breath and voice.
All I have is a tablet I opened on my brother's desk,
written repeatedly "he is not my father," then "he is not my"
then "he is not" then "he is" then "he" then nothing nothing
nothing nothing…..
that megaphone blaring a silence loud as a carnie barker calling
you in
so he can guess your weight, your age, your rage.

What do you do? The table is set, the plates sprawled out,
the napkins with their legs unfolded,
the silverware huddling together,
the food on its back….we gotta eat.

Tell the guesser he has been fooled
and you have won that stuffed animal……
14, 136 and pi, propelled by absolutely no pattern or reason.

Father was weak,
slunk in on his belly,
arms retracted, legs recoiled.

Mother set water to boil.

My sister fanned herself with a *National Geographic*
soon to be pleated pages, the robe of a felt-winged
Christmas angel.

My brother faced our old Zenith,
which stared back at him
like a fan aghast at her idol close-up.

Outside in blizzard,
snow lifted itself and fell
over and over, the only available resurrection for miles.
I could best count the pleasure I had
being in this family
if my hand were a stump.

22

When the hand can no longer
stand to hold the knife,
the meals have been dispersed from boxes,
our hair shorn like curtains ripped down,
our mother seemed proudest,
pearls to the bite of the bodice of her dress,
her stockings thin sheaths to legs long as planets.

I knew then, tipsy as I was on bark or drink,
deluded by histories
I'd begun to spell in new languages,
I knew that as she carried me once,
she still did but as secret or lie,
that the corners of her room could tell me her ache.

A mother is a woman
who believes she gave birth to you,
that through the miracle of spoons
you were fed even though once you were all mouth;
you've got the decorum of lips as of late and
this is it.

She could not sing but was your lullaby,
nonetheless, like a priest whispering
in the dark. You must absolve all of her sins,
even if the worst is you.

See her over there lingering by that door
as though she were blind.
She is not blind and you remember that.

Mother tended our sweetness
with her wooden spoon.
Sometimes, when she crouched,
we gathered at the hem of her skirt,
like stitches
We rolled in our tongues then our speech
on which we'd hung our sentences
to be blown dry by the temporary winds
given us.

I remember the spigot
of her mouth,
the small feet of my sisters, the sun's
unction on my shoulders.
I was certain my mother
said everything she thought.
Later, I was wrong.

24

Obsessed with the cantos of dawn,
our mother gave up sleep
as if it were a bad habit during Lent.
She hovered and waited and stilled herself,
so she might translate morning
not the glory of sun
or the demise of dark,
rather the bringing from back to front to font
what night had covered.
Can't we simply hold her now?

And our father who died when his son/not-son
buckled to the river, who stopped sculling
with his arms, the underwater propulsion of
his feet like a unicycle rider on a tight rope,
whatever killed him as merciful as the Pieta,
Mary carrying her Jesus against gravity.
We can only hold our holding of me,
make a just act, a *mot juste* so clear
the universe has no need to decipher it.

Because I want to capitulate, reclaim
my love of water, that when I'm in it,
be it bath or lake…yes even river,
my skin is a giving barrier between
the waters of self and what's beyond.

25

How to remember a love song
is before, when all we knew
was dream when mouths of rivers
meant only to kiss us, slick as fish passing through current as
currents passed through us, then.
When no breaths were ever sinister and land between two rivers merely
a woman's body lying in its own western edges,
sun slurping moisture from her hips.

We waded into our waters,
our fins dissolving whispers,
our gills gone,
carried downstream but not missed.

Whoever heard that red clatter just then,
as if the horizon were being pulled apart,
whoever that was
we didn't believe him and we were wrong;
go back to even before that. Please.

I should have known "I think you
dropped an earring on the floor" was a goodbye
that said "Sweet sister, suicide is redundant."

Versed as I am in the way language clots
like gravy thickening.

I should have guessed that the faucet dripping
that morning after my brother left the kitchen
was foreshadowing of larger water,
deeper basins.

I should have realized the first time I remembered
going into my own sleep in the privacy only a child knows
might be a symbol I'd always want to tease from its perch.

What I didn't understand is that I would always have this,
open-eyed or closed...

Thank You

Thank you to Larry Woiwode and Judsom Mitcham, great teachers and great writers. Kudos to Brent Goodman and Lurlynn Franklin for their generosity and encouragement. I am indebted to many poets I've never met whose work has repeatedly connected me to the possibilities of a poetry, most importantly Mark Strand and his poem, "Keeping Things Whole." This poem has saved my psyche on more than one occasion.

Thank you to photographer Joshua Earle for making some of his photos available for use for free under a very generous Creative Commons License. His adapted photograph is the cover for this collection.

I am grateful beyond words to my parents for their hard work, patience and love. Thank you also to my brother and sister for their continuing support. And for my husband, who pushes me, consoles me, challenges me and supports me, I can only offer up the word, "love," even though it is incomplete in describing what we create together.

Nancy Devine, a three-time Pushcart Prize nominee, is a writer whose poetry, short fiction and essays have appeared in a number of online and print literary magazines and journals, including *Bellevue Literary Review, Midwestern Gothic-A Literary Journal, Stirring-A Literary Collection, Berfois, Referential Magazine* and *Hermeneutic Chaos Literary Journal*. She loves to cook, garden, and figure things out. She teaches high school English in Grand Forks, North Dakota, where she lives with her husband and their rambunctious rescue collie.